READY ~ SET ~ NEXT: Moving Forward by Embracing Your Past & Empowering Your Future

Barbara Schiffman

Published by Barbara Schiffman, 2023.

While every precaution has been taken in the preparation of this book, the publisher assumes no responsibility for errors or omissions, or for damages resulting from the use of the information contained herein.

READY ~ SET ~ NEXT: MOVING FORWARD BY EMBRACING YOUR PAST & EMPOWERING YOUR FUTURE

First edition. August 4, 2023.

ISBN: 979-8223231394

Written by Barbara Schiffman.

Table of Contents

To Glenn, who has taken many leaps of faith with me.

~~~~~~

This book was previously published as a Kindle Vella (serialized).

~~~~~

Contact Barbara Schiffman at www.LiteraSee.com

1 ~ Insights in Hindsight

"This is a new year. A new beginning. And things will change." - Taylor Swift

AUGUST, 2023 - Whitefish MT: It's been almost ten years since I wrote the introduction below. The whole world changed dramatically since then – with many endings, new beginnings and unexpected shifts for all of us.

Five years ago this month (2018) I began preparing for what I hoped would be the final "big shift" in my life: moving from Los Angeles to Northwest Montana to be closer to my daughter and grandkids.

Four years ago my husband, my cat and I arrived in Montana to live here full-time. It was time for us to spend our days closer to our growing grandkids. I marvel each day at how fast those years flew by. I've learned more about endings, new beginnings and what it really takes to move forward in life than I'd expected.

And we've all learned a lot more about patience, resilience and surrender in our collective lives as humanity continues to confront post-Covid and other challenges that seem to be holding us hostage. I prefer to think these societal challenges are bringing us closer together (or will do so as we embrace them...)

I invite you to read the original introduction to this "workshop in a book" I wrote in 2012—when I first shared it with my Life&Soul Synergy students. I originally created this **Ready Set Next** toolkit to help me move from 2012 to 2013.

Since then, I've revised the processes and use them now to stay grounded in my "new normal." I hope you will try out these exercises and meditations to begin creating a new foundation for your present and future as well.

CHRISTMAS DAY, 2012 - Los Angeles CA: This month we've all begun anew even before New Year's Eve arrives. We turned the last page on the Mayan calendar on 12/21/12 and survived what some people consider the end of an evolutionary cycle.

As we move into a new year, we're still collectively facing national and global challenges, healing from unspeakable tragedies and crises, and seeking more clarity about what's to come. But as we continue to move forward though this challenging year, new milestones appear, day by day.

Moving forward always requires courage, intuition and guidance. Our mission as humans seems to be to continue evolving, no matter what happens around us.

Personally, I've encountered more milestones in the past two months than during the prior ten months of 2012. I weathered the most challenging weeks of my husband's recovery after he broke his leg on 11/11/12. This unexpected "mishap" dramatically slowed both of us down and made moving in any direction—forward or back—extremely literal and slow for him. It also made me conscious of the effort it takes to get things done every day, both for him and for me.

As I reflect back on 2012, these key moments are already shaping my life. This book is based on a Life Balance workshop I developed and taught over the past decade. The workshop was inspired by classes I've taken from others, books I've read, and a radio episode I produced for my "Living in Balance" internet show which aired Christmas week 2007.

This particular blend of "inner support" tools has come full circle (pun intended) through my sharing it with you. I've designed the processes, explorations and meditations to help you move forward from wherever you are to whatever's next at any time of the year or any phase of your life.

My hope is you'll use these processes (or at least the ones that resonate at the time) whenever you need a *fresh start or energy boost*.

New Year's is an obvious time for new beginnings - we all hope the next year will be better than the last, or at least as good if we liked what occurred in our life and in the world. But so are birthdays, anniversaries, graduations, new moons, new jobs, new relationships, new homes, new friendships, new projects - i.e., any event that has significance in your unique and precious life.

Whenever you feel a need to move on, or at least a few steps forward from where you've been, I invite you to get **Ready and Set** by creating a clean slate. Then leap powerfully into whatever's **Next** for you.

BEFORE WE MOVE ON:

Think about your life a year ago—where were you, what were you doing, how were you feeling? And here you are now—where, with whom, feeling how?

We think time passes around us, but it's actually moving *through* us, changing our cells, our thoughts and our feelings. We can start over at any time—we're always in control of our own lives at the thinking and feeling levels.

People are usually focused on what happened in the past (or what didn't happen) and fail to sense what might be ahead, "just around the corner" so to speak.

Please be aware that the processes I'll share with you are not about finding fault or blame, analyzing or rationalizing, or absolving yourself (or anyone else) from responsibility for how things really are. But if we can face the unknown with joy in our hearts - or at least some curiosity - no matter what has happened in our lives so far, the unexpected can occur and the future can become an adventure!

As Sarah Ban Breathnach, author of *Simple Abundance* (and one of my personal teachers) wrote: "Begin today. Declare out loud to the universe that you are willing to let go of struggle and eager to learn through joy." *I invite you to start now...*

2 ~ Pausing at the Crossroads...

"The secret to a rich life is to have more beginnings than endings."
- Dave Weinbaum

MOST PEOPLE OPERATE on what I think of as "machine-time." They're tethered 24/7 to electronic devices for the constant flow of information, even when they're sleeping.

We're all neurologically overloaded *(I call it "infowhelmed")*. This is due to the abundance of data we receive and send around the clock via portable devices, computers, televisions and radios, as well as by word of mouth from and to co-workers, friends and family. It's easy to get exhausted just thinking about it!

Our minds are getting even more crowded with data - some that's truly important and a lot more that's totally irrelevant - with each passing year. In 2005, marketing expert and best selling author Dave Lakhani observed that we received more mental and visual input *in one day* than our great-grandparents in 1900 absorbed *in a year.*

In September 2009, analysts from Basex, a knowledge-economy research firm, gave a report at the world's first web-conference designed to honor "Information Overload Day." The report claimed that humans were creating more content *each day* than "an entire population of the planet could consume *in a month*," due to the rapid growth of YouTube, Twitter, Facebook, podcasts, blogs and web-TV.

In December 2009, only a few months later, a University of California, San Diego, study reported that on average, each individual consumes about 34 gigabytes of data and information *each day* - an increase of about *350 percent* since the 1980s!

Can you imagine how much our daily info-input has multiplied *by now*, with the constant barrage of infotainment and mental clutter we receive on dozens of devices each hour? I can't. And even though our bodies were in "lockdown" in 2020, our minds were plugged in online, Zooming and Facebooking more hours each day than ever before in our lives. Some of us have stayed plugged in ever since...

So it's no wonder few people make time to take stock of what's going on in their lives. They're too busy adding new information to their memory banks to stop and review what's already in there. Taking a pause to review what's been accomplished, what's still unfinished &/or what's next seems to be the domain of statistical analysts and business forecasters.

Individuals also tend to drift through life rather than experience it with conscious awareness. When we take time to reflect on the past, most of us do so on birthdays, anniversaries or New Year's Day. But we're often so *infowhelmed* that we prefer to look ahead rather than gain *insight through hindsight*.

Life coaches (like me) can be helpful in breaking this pattern. Before they begin to make significant changes, we often ask our clients to evaluate the elements of their lives, personal and professional, and create a "snapshot" of where they're at now. This makes them more aware of and accountable for their progress - or lack of it - as they take actions to accomplish a tangible goal.

As your personal Life Balance Coach through this book, I want you to be aware that we're going to do something similar in the **Ready Set Next** process. But whether you have a tangible goal or not doesn't matter here. Our **Ready Set Next** goal is to begin to *evolve consciously* as we move forward in our lives day by day.

We'll begin by **REVIEWING a time period** that's relevant to *what's ending in your life right now:* you can choose a year, a month, a moon cycle, a relationship, a job, a phase of your personal growth, or whatever's true for you.

This will create perspective - a broader viewpoint from which to evaluate where you're at - as well as *anchor you* properly in the past you've lived so far. Your past got you here - it had and has Purpose. We'll explore that more later...

As you look back over a finite time period of your choice, you will be able to see how you got here more clearly than by just thinking about "the past" in general and rather vague terms. But this is not a blame-game, and you shouldn't have "done it better" or differently. If you could have, you would have.

I believe you're *exactly* where you need to be, even if it doesn't look the way you hoped it would. We'll be scouting for signs of *progress* - even an inch counts . We'll notice the "good stuff" you've accomplished in this finite time period – that includes *internal shifts* as well as tangible results.

After we make note of the good, we'll peek at the other stuff. This includes tangible &/or emotional baggage you are still dragging around despite your desire to leave it behind. Then you will be ready to objectively *choose what to let go* — including old obligations, unfinished projects &/or unsatisfying relationships.

Releasing your attachment to what drains you allows you to *commit anew,* from a place of personal power, to activities and people that can enhance your future.

This conscious **Review, Release and Recommit process** is simple yet amazingly effective. It literally shifts your energy from the inside out by honoring your past. It also helps you detach the stagnant energy of what no longer serves you (people, places, beliefs, objects, feelings, and more) with gratitude and appreciation.

BUT BEFORE WE MOVE on:

I know, I know - you want to get right to "the good stuff" already - but there's not much room in your "inner space" (subconscious or conscious) for the good stuff until you clear out some of the clutter and junk.

Think of your closets or garage or storage units - how full are they today? How recently have you looked in the boxes parked there? Keep in mind that Releasing is just as important as Receiving—you can't do one without doing the other. Hang in there and stick with me - the results will be worth it!

"LIFE IS NOT MADE UP of minutes, hours, days, weeks, months, or years, but of moments. You must experience each one before you can appreciate it." - Sarah Ban Breathnach

Shaping Where We're Going by Seeing Where We've Been

3 ~ Step One: Questions, Learnings & Themes

"Time has no divisions to mark its passage, there is never a thunderstorm or blare of trumpets to announce the beginning of a new month or year. Even when a new century begins it is only we mortals who ring bells and fire pistols." - Thomas Mann

WELCOME TO YOUR RECENT-PAST REVIEW:

Every journey starts at the first stepping stone. Our first step, however, is to *pause* and look back at how we got here before we move ahead.

This helps us clean the slate and reclaim as much of our energy that's still stuck to the past as we can. Then it will be ready to use for something newer, better and definitely more fun.

You don't need to ruminate about the past all day - 30 minutes or so is plenty of time for your **Recent Past Review**. *(If you take time, it's okay, but don't get stuck there...)*

TO GET READY:

Have your most recent calendar or DayPlanner handy (on your phone or tablet or a tangible version).

Get a notebook and pen or pencil (you may want to erase and rewrite a bit) - or open a new document on your computer.

Put on some music, especially songs or types of music that help you focus.

You can also light a candle if you wish.

Then set a timer for **30 minutes.**

We'll start by **Reviewing the PAST YEAR** - or, if you're not reading this during New Year's week, you can Review the months which have passed since the current year began.

Note: After you practice the Review process by looking back over the current or just-passed calendar year, you'll be able to Review any time-period that's relevant to your Fresh Start - like the length of your last project, job, relationship or marriage, etc.

SINCE WE'RE LOOKING at specific time periods or years in our lives, I'm reminded of a quote by dramatist and author Zora Neale Hurston:

"There are years that ask questions and years that answer."

If your past year (or other time period) was full of **Questions,** let's begin by listing any of those Questions that still need answers. *(This might even help the rest of this new year or time period to Answer them as it unfolds.)*

Pause here to write your Questions list, then continue...

"TOMORROW IS THE MOST important thing in life. Comes into us at midnight very clean. It's perfect when it arrives and it puts itself in our hands. It hopes we've learned something from yesterday." - John Wayne

I LIKE HOW JOHN WAYNE suggests that our Future "hopes we've learned" something from our Past. That way we don't have to repeat it... *right?*

In each year of our lives, as well as in each decade, I believe we **learn** something new. We're not usually aware of what we're learning while we're in the middle of the lesson, however, and sometimes we notice new meanings long after the lesson ends.

Think about what you've learned from the past year and make a list of those Learnings.

THEMES can also be a *combination of words* that individually and collectively embody the feeling, energy or "flavor" of the year or time period.

I like to use two or three words, especially if they offer alliteration (i.e. they all start with the same letter or have a similar sound). This makes my Theme rhythmic so it's easier to remember and feels good on my tongue when I say it.

My 2012 Theme, for example, was "Delighted and Delicious." When choices, actions or opportunities arose during that year, I'd deliberately notice if they made me feel "delighted" or "delicious" - or both.

If so, I'd make the choice or take the action; if not, I'd see if there was a way to make the choice or action more delightful or delicious so that I could.

If you like music, see if you can come up with a Song that contains a good theme for your year or time period.

Take a pause here to write down your Theme (or Theme Song)...

"NOTHING IS PREDESTINED. The obstacles of your past can become the gateways that lead to new beginnings." -Ralph Blum

NEXT, WE'LL REVIEW your **Accomplishments** - to evaluate and honor what went right. Our lives can look different in hindsight when we look at ourselves as heroes in our own journey. Then the Questions, Learnings and Themes get clearer and feel better as stepping stones taking us forward, helping us evolve and even enjoy the journey.

Did any of your Questions, Learnings or Themes give you a new perspective on your life this past year. If yes, that's great. If not, hang in there - more will be revealed as we explore your past year's Accomplishments...

4 ~ Your Accomplishments

*"*N*ew Year's Day is every man's birthday." ~ Charles Lamb*

NOW IT'S TIME TO GO deeper with our **Review**. When you look back over your past year (or other time period), do you notice mostly *what went wrong or what went right?*

As we know, optimists generally see what worked well while pessimists notice the problems, failures and unfinished business.

Journalist Ellen Goodman wrote: "We spend January first walking through our lives, room by room, drawing up a list of work to be done, cracks to be patched. Maybe this year, to balance the list, we ought to walk through the rooms of our lives... not looking for flaws, but for potential."

In her final Washington Post column on 1/1/2010, Goodman also quoted something she had written 30 years earlier that I believe is relevant to getting Ready and Set for whatever's Next:

"There's a trick to the Graceful Exit. It begins with the vision to recognize when a job, a life stage, a relationship is over - and to let go. It means leaving what's over without denying its validity or its past importance in our lives. It involves a sense of future, a belief that every exit line is an entry, that we are moving on rather than out."

In the next phase of our Review, let's look for the "past importance" in what happened over your year (or other time period) as well as any "potentials" you can see.

"CHEERS TO A NEW YEAR and another chance for us to get it right." - Oprah Winfrey

WE'LL REVIEW YOUR *Accomplishments*, which include but are not limited to what most people would identify as *Achievements*.

Achievements are often seen as *tangible results* while accomplishments can also be an *internal shift* that you feel even if nothing appears to have changed externally.

For example, not getting upset by someone in your life who has long pushed your emotional buttons is an accomplishment - you can feel it even though no one else can see it. That makes it a very big deal!

Getting the laundry done on a weekly basis or making your bed every day can be an accomplishment (and an achievement), especially if you have a busy schedule. It can also add order to your life.

Having more fun more often can be a huge accomplishment for workaholics - as can getting more done with less hesitation or effort if you tend to procrastinate.

Know that whatever *feels* like an accomplishment to you *is one*. No one else can judge or choose this for you.

If it's true for you, it matters. If it made a difference for you, appreciate it and take credit. It will always be a part of you, and may prove to be essential to your forward movement from now on.

In your Notes, **LIST all the things you Accomplished** during the past year (or other time period):

Try to list *one or more* accomplishments from each of these categories:

- your career or work
- your family
- your friendships
- your business relationships • your personal growth
- your creative projects (for work or just for fun)
- your self-care and fun time *(what's that, you may wonder?)*
- your health
- your motivations and goals
- your wishes, hopes and dreams (think "bucket list"!)

Don't worry if you can't think of accomplishments for all of these categories - the ones that are truly important will stand out.

LOOK OVER YOUR CALENDAR to jog your memory. Page through the months - notice what occurred when. In some cases, they're ongoing; in others they're specific to a particular month or event.

You don't need to list your accomplishments in chronological order - just add them to the list as you think of them. When they occurred isn't as important (in most cases) as the fact that you're claiming them as accomplishments!

Take a pause here to write your Accomplishments, then continue...

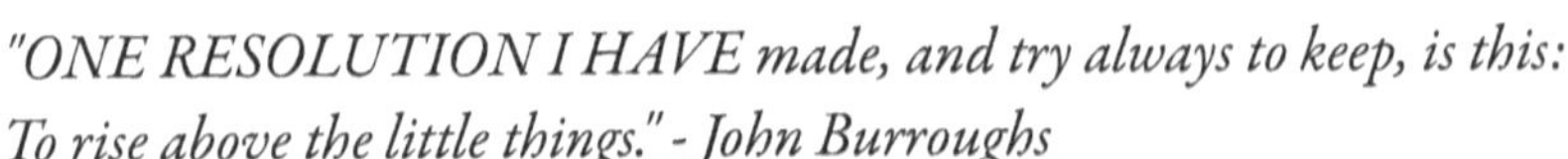

"ONE RESOLUTION I HAVE made, and try always to keep, is this: To rise above the little things." - John Burroughs

NOW REVIEW YOUR LIST as you ask yourself the questions below in relation to the past year (or other relevant period or event). Write down whatever comes to mind:

- What was the best thing that happened to you?
- What are you really proud about?
- What did you create?
- What did you accomplish *internally?*
- What did you accomplish *tangibly?*
- Who did you really help?
- Who do you need to thank or acknowledge for being there for you?
- Who did you meet that's now important in your life?
- What do you want to be acknowledged for most - even if others might not consider it a big deal?

Pause here to make notes on these questions &/or add to your list of Accomplishments

"DON'T CRY BECAUSE ITS over, smile because it happened." - Dr. Seuss

WOW! LOOK AT WHAT YOU'VE accomplished! The accomplishments I remember and feel the most are those that are or were *internal* - shifting how I responded to people and events rather than "reacting" to them as if they were intended to hurt me. Helping a lot of people with a word, a smile, an hour of my time.

Who you are is as important as *what you do.* Just being YOU is a big accomplishment - never forget that!

We'll continue to clear space in the next section by making our "inner clutter" tangible (in lists.) Then we'll be ready to let some of that clutter go, easily and effortlessly, through ***visualization***!

5 ~ Unfinished Business

"M*aybe it's not always trying to fix something broken; maybe it's about starting over and creating something better." - Anonymous*

LIFE IS A BLEND OF The Good, The Bad and The Ugly. While we all like the good stuff, we're often too close to the bad and the ugly stuff to see the glimmers of good within them too. Most challenges contain "golden nuggets" that can help us move forward and empower us to do things differently from now on.

Now that we've acknowledged some of the "good stuff" from the past year (or your chosen time period), let's take a brief look at some of the "other stuff" in your life. That includes your **Unfinished Business!**

I promise that this look at what's Unfinished won't hurt - it will even be cathartic and empowering. So you won't and can't use it as another way to beat yourself up.

We all have Unfinished Business in our lives. Life is essentially a juggling act. Something's always getting started, other things are in progress, and some things keep lingering because we haven't yet finished them off properly and let them go. (This can include choosing *not* to finish them, by the way!)

START A NEW LIST so you can review and consider the items, projects, events or other things in your life today that *feel incomplete or unfinished.* This means they're still nagging at your thoughts, keeping you up at night &/or showing up on your daily or weekly to-do lists.

These items might be projects you're working on, emails you need to send, phone calls you need to return, something you need to tell someone that you've been avoiding. All of these things are draining your energy.

Your thoughts feel real but they're actually not - at the moment they're only taking up valuable mind-space that you can use for better thoughts and projects. So let's see which "mental space-stealers" can get cleared out of your mind today.

IN *"Write It Down, Make It Happen"* - a book I recommend for Forward Movers like you - author Henriette Anne Klauser explores how writing things down gets them out of your head and helps clarify what you really want &/or need.

If you've read books about the Law of Attraction, you're aware of how writing things down also helps raise your energy to equal the wavelength of the things you desire. This in turn helps attract them to you - or you to them - much more easily and quickly. Making your thoughts tangible has an *alchemical impact* that reaches far beyond logic and reason.

Writing things down *by hand* also generates a stronger vibration than typing them on a computer, tablet or smart phone. What science calls an **ideomotor response** actually creates a neuro-connection between our hands and our subconscious minds when we write words via pen or pencil (even if your handwriting is hard to read).

Making a list in your own handwriting instead of typing it actually stimulates and creates powerful neuro-pathways. This tends to be true whether we're writing things we want to keep track of, things we want to release or things we want to magnetize. As the words go through our fingers onto paper, they become tangible and active.

FOR NOW, LISTING *what's Unfinished* for you may also feel frustrating because you can't finish all the items right away. But this is not an exercise to point out what's wrong in your life.

There's actually *nothing* wrong. What's Unfinished for you are just good intentions - including goals, plans, projects, people and events - that you're not ready or able to complete and release, at least not yet...

Wouldn't you prefer to create mental and emotional freedom for *what's next* in your life instead of continuing to drag around a long to-do list? Imagine it's a suitcase filled with rocks - it will exhaust you and keep you from moving quickly.

After we Review what's Unfinished, you'll feel so much lighter. In fact, you'll be able to make fresh choices based on what's true for you *today*, not last week or last month or last year.

THINK ABOUT THESE AREAS of your life again:

- Career or work...

- Your family and other relationships...
- Personal growth...
- Health and fitness...
- Travel...
- Fun and hobbies...
- Your short-term and long-term goals...
- Your wishes and dreams.

As you did with *Accomplishments*, write down whatever comes to mind in the order you think of the items.

You can refer to your calendar and current to-do list to help you identify what's still Unfinished - notice what's still taking up space in your calendar (as well as your mind and your life).

If this process makes you feel anxious or resistant, **take some deep breaths...**

"Failure is the opportunity to begin again more intelligently." - *Henry Ford*

Now pause here and write down your Unfinished items, get them out of your head and onto the page.

A NOTE FOR LIST MAKERS like me:

I make lists of the things I need to do almost every day (including my Unfinished Business &/or New Projects and Tasks).

When I use up or run out of items, I make lists of what I need to get at the store. When I'm ready to run errands, I make lists of the stores and other places I need to go (like the library).

I occasionally make Master Lists of my short term and long term projects, tasks and "good ideas." This gives me an *overview* of what's relevant in my life at the time.

I love how good it feels to cross off items as they get done. If they stay on the list too long, I cross them off when I decide they're no longer useful or relevant.

We'll be doing that soon in our Ready Set Next process as we begin to make space for What's Next. So be sure to put ALL of your Unfinished Business on your review list. I promise it will feel great to cross off your Unfinished items as they get completed. And you'll learn several ways that you can complete them...

6 ~ Beginning to Let Go

Congratulations! You survived the most difficult part of the **Ready Set Next** Process: listing things that are dragging you down.

Now you can decide which ones you can *let go of!* This includes anything that feels okay even if it remains unfinished or unsaid.

Cross these items off your list now - and notice how liberating this feels.

If you find it painful or challenging to cross out some items, remember that you can always choose to finish those items or say those things to the right person *later* even if you cross them off your list *for now*.

Letting go of as many unfinished items as possible creates more mental and emotional space. This also empowers you to address the items you can't let go of now but still really want to work on or finish as you move into your new year, new phase, new life.

Take a few minutes to cross o! every item you're ready to let go of on your Unfinished list, then we'll continue...

GREAT! NOW NOTICE HOW many items you crossed off. It may be a dozen, or just one - *or possibly none.*

Going through the process of *evaluating, choosing and eliminating* them is what counts. This also gives you practice in **Reviewing and taking action** instead of just running on automatic like usual.

Once you've crossed off every item on your list that you honestly can, take another breath - or have a piece of chocolate if you need a yummy reward. You've earned it!

But we're not quite done with this list yet. We still need to Review the items that remain on your Unfinished list: *the ones you just can't let go of... yet.*

It's okay - we all have them. Just notice what yours are and view them with fresh eyes if you can.

Are there any items you can actually finish in the coming week? If so, make a big "X" beside them on your list.

Then write down a *date* beside each item which indicates when you think you can have it finished - the week, day, or even the hour.

In your calendar, also make a note about each of these items on the day you have chosen for it to be finished. This makes it real on your personal timeline and takes it out of your head.

Be sure to consider *how much time may be needed* to finish each item as you put it in your calendar. Schedule this in before its "due date" so it won't still be on your Unfinished list a year from now!

Here's a big tip: Make note of the **first step(s)** you'll need to take to finish each item.

Taking the *first step* usually makes the next step clearer and easier, and helps you keep taking one step at a time until suddenly it's done!

Now ask yourself if you feel **complete** with these items - that means you feel okay about them even though they're not yet finished or said.

They're still on your list, but they're okay just as they are *for now.* This lets them stay on your list without you feeling guilty or resistant to finishing them.

If there's anything else on your list that's still nagging at you, make note of it now so you can return to it later. By then it may no longer need attention - or it may have miraculously gotten finished or resolved without much effort.

If not, you'll likely be able to decide what you can do about it when you're not feeling pressured. Those "loose ends" won't go anywhere without you!

Take a few minutes if needed to review and address *any other items* remaining on your Unfinished list, then we'll continue...

ARE YOU FEELING LIGHTER now that you've let some of your Unfinished Business go? Do you feel more complete and satisfied?

Our next step will be a **Guided Meditation** incorporating NLP (neuro- linguistic programming). These techniques will help your subconscious and internal support systems *integrate* the liberating energy of the work you've been doing so far.

This is all preparation for moving powerfully into your future...

7 ~ Inner Journey to Appreciate & Release Your Past

You've been making lists and Reviewing your past year (or chosen period) and are now ready to continue Moving Forward...

First, set all of your written lists aside - but keep some note paper and a pen handy. You'll need them for notes after we do some Inner Visualization, our 5th step in the *Ready Set Next* process.

To fully honor your past, we'll do some guided meditations using NLP (neuro-linguistic programming) techniques to synchronize and amplify your subconscious and internal support systems.

Start by closing your door, putting your phone on mute (or off) and setting aside time where you definitely won't be disturbed. Make sure you have at least 10-15 minutes to yourself - *but you're welcome to go slower and take more time if you wish...*

YOU CAN *read* **the following meditation processes to yourself as you go through them &/or** *record* **them (on your phone or tablet) for playback:**

Get comfortable and close your eyes - take some deep breaths - let yourself "just be" in this moment.

Everything you want to do, finish, complete, or begin will wait for you while you're doing some inner releasing.

Now think about your PAST and notice *where* you **sense your Past coming from in your** *Inner Timeline* – does it come from behind you, the left or right side, above you, below you - or maybe from in front of you.

Also notice where you **sense your Future is going** - it may be the opposite side of your Past.

Or it may be going toward a different side or up or down and doesn't make a straight line with your Past. That's fine...

However it feels is **just right for you**. There's no right way to feel and sense your personal *Inner Timeline* - take whatever comes to mind first - ***and just breathe...***

Now, in your mind's eye, let yourself *float up over your Timeline* and then gently *float back into your Past* - down through the past year (or as far as you need to go to release whatever you're completing today)...

As you float, just breathe...

Notice a **glowing giant pearl** on your Timeline which ***represents an event*** that feels to you like an Accomplishment from this past year (or other chosen time period).

Let yourself ***look down into the pearl*** - see yourself within the pearl as if you're on a TV or movie screen.

See yourself *within your Accomplishment,* whatever it might be.

See what you saw... feel what you felt... hear what you heard...

Let the *energy of your Accomplishment* surround and embrace you as it unfolds within the pearl. Absorb this energy into your body.

Let this empowering energy stay with you as you gently ***move back toward NOW,*** bringing a stronger sense of this particular Accomplishment into your Present and also your Future.

Now *float up and over your Timeline* until you're hovering over the space that feels like *NOW*.

Notice that there's a **balloon** floating right next to you - it may be slighting above you. Whatever color or shape or pattern your balloon has is just right.

This balloon holds the *energy* of all the things you're now ready to *release* from your past year (or time period you're working with today).

This can include to-do lists, people, relationships, projects, words that you said, words you didn't say but wish you had, places you went or didn't go but wish you had—anything that can now be released...

You don't need to sense or see each piece of this Unfinished Business - just sense that *all the things* you truly don't want to carry with you into your Future are now being held energetically within this balloon.

Grab the string dangling from the balloon and just breathe.

Take several breaths and gently (or forcefully if you prefer) *blow* your breath into the balloon.

Let all the energy of whatever's still unfinished for you *move out of your body and into the balloon* through your breath.

Notice that the balloon gently expands with each breath.

Blow or just breathe into this balloon until it's full. *Then stop.*

Now count to 3—when you get to 3 *let go of the balloon*: **1 - 2 - 3. Let go!**

Notice how easily the balloon floats up and away from you - further and further and further – and even further - until you can't see it anymore.

How does it feel to easily let go of all the things you released into the balloon?

You can do this anytime you need to let go of things - close your eyes and breathe them into an "inner balloon" **and just let go**.

Trust that they will be transformed and taken care of by the Universe after you release them.

Now - gently float above your Inner Timeline again, landing gently in NOW.

Take 3 deep breaths to bring you back into your body... into your personal space and time... to help you get grounded in the Present .

When you're ready, open your eyes.

WELCOME BACK! TAKE a few minutes to make notes about what you saw or experienced during this Inner Visualization - especially what was new, insightful or meaningful for you.

Before we take *another inner journey* to gain more insights about your Past and also receive *some gifts that can be helpful to you* in your Future, be sure to *ground yourself:* drink some water, stand up and stretch, pet your dog or cat, or even take a bathroom break...

WHEN YOU'RE READY, let's continue...

Close your eyes and get comfortable again.

Take some deep breaths and let yourself "just be" in this moment.

Now reconnect with your Inner Timeline - **sense your Past and Future directions again.**

Float up over your Timeline and glide over the Past to another **glowing pearl** – one that contains an item on your **ACCOMPLISHMENTS** list.

Whichever one you come to first is the right one.

Look down on this Accomplishment pearl - *see who's there, where it is, what's happening...*

Notice if someone is acknowledging you for this particular Accomplishment. *If so, how does that feel?*

If by some chance no one else is with you in that Accomplishment pearl, or if it is an Internal Accomplishment or something that happened with no one else around, ***acknowledge yourself!***

Feel the acknowledgement - notice where the feeling goes in your body.

Take a deep breath and let it in.

When you're ready, float to another glowing pearl on your Past Timeline - one that's *unfinished* or at least still nagging at you.

Is it one of the things you can't let go of?

Ask yourself: What's the **LESSON** in this for you?

Get the Learning from it NOW - take a few moments to receive it.

You don't need to "figure it out" - just see it, feel it, allow it in...

If you can't get the Learning easily, try floating a bit higher above your Timeline and *look down on it* - do you get some hint of a message from this item or experience?

If nothing comes after a few moments, let yourself trust that the Learning will come to you later, probably in your everyday life - *maybe even in your dreams tonight.*

If you do get a new understanding or Learning about this, just breathe it in and feel it settle into your body.

Where does it go - how does it feel?

Look down again at the pearl containing the event or item - see if the event or item feels different, perhaps more finished than before?

When you're ready, glide back to NOW...

Breathe in to **anchor** all the things you did last year... all the things you learned or experienced that enhance you at both the human level and the Soul level.

Sense them even if you don't know what they are yet.

Take 3 more deep breaths to gently reconnect with your body... with your personal space and time.

When you're ready, open your eyes.

Make notes about what you saw or experienced during this Inner Journey - especially anything that was new, insightful or meaningful for you.

DID YOU ENJOY YOUR visualization and Inner Journey? Did you notice several Accomplishment Pearls on your Timeline? Did you let go of stuck energy connected to Unfinished Business?

Even if you can't feel it yet, I'm sure you've received fresh understandings or useful learnings - and also released some or all of the stuck "unfinished" energy.

By acknowledging at least some of your Accomplishments, you've created more clear mind-body space. This will help you feel and express more of your own positive energy in your life. Let it support you and energize you.

Now you're ready to move forward and empower what's NEXT for you...

Envisioning Your Future & Empowering Your Whole Life

8 ~ Looking Ahead

"Tomorrow is the first blank page of a 365 page book. Write a good one." - Brad Paisley

LET'S SWITCH GEARS and begin moving forward into the New Year (or whatever time period you're working on).

Your "new year" can begin whenever you want because *every day* offers you a fresh start.

I like how, in the quote above, country singer Brad Paisley thinks of tomorrow as a "blank page" of a year-long book and urges you to "write a good one"!

Let's begin by resetting your timer for another 30 minutes.

Then take your notebook or computer and, on a new blank page, list some ***things you'd like to do or accomplish*** in the coming year.

If it's not New Year's week at the moment, think ahead to *a year from now.* This will give you plenty of time to accomplish the things on your new "To Do Next" list - plus those you'll soon be envisioning! Then you won't have an Unfinished list to review a year from now...

If you're not sure where to begin, start by *listing items you've chosen to carry over* from last year's Unfinished list. Since the stuck energy of your past has been released - or at least loosened up - think of ways you can make each one feel fresh and exciting again as you write these items anew on your "To Do Next" list.

If they make you think of brand new items that can benefit from all the energy you'll have once the Unfinished items are finally finished, list those new items too!

Knowing you'll continue adding to this list from now on, take a few minutes to write down every item you can think of that you'd like to Accomplish.

Then add the ones you've chosen to finish this coming year.

Now grab your calendar and write some of these "To Do Next" items *in your calendar* during the months or weeks you'd like for them to be complete.

If they're ongoing projects or events, writing them in your calendar will make them "real" as part of your ongoing activities, not just part of your thoughts. This will prevent them from taking up extra mind-space you can use for other projects and accomplishments.

Keep in mind that writing things down helps make them happen....

Take a few minutes to write these items in your calendar...

"The object of a new year is not that we should have a new year. It is that we should have a new soul." ~ G.K. Chesterton

NOW THINK ABOUT A **THEME** for your New Year!

Since you're not looking back in hindsight like we did before to see what themes or patterns are in your Past, you truly have a clean slate to *choose any theme you want!*

What Theme would make you feel excited about the coming year, like my 2012 "Delicious and Delighted" theme did for me?

Since that was the Theme I chose at the start of the year, not one I saw as my year's theme in hindsight, it gave me an energy boost all year long. It also served as my benchmark for choices, actions and states of being along the way.

Know that your Theme is not locked in stone once you choose it at this new starting point. It can and likely will evolve, especially if this is the first time you're consciously choosing a Theme for your foreseeable future.

Since it's *your* Theme, you can change or adjust it any time you want! It needs to benefit and work for you, not make you feel stuck or guilty.

With that in mind, I came up with a Theme Song for 2013 that supported my optimism and excitement for the energy of the new year. The song ***"(I Had) The Time of My Life"*** from the movie *Dirty Dancing* suddenly started playing in my mind one day. I realized that's how I wanted to feel *every* day - like I'm having the Time of My Life. So I chose it as my Theme Song for that year.

If a potential Theme Song pops into your mind too, try what I did: I chose the song version I liked best on iTunes (or wherever you get your music) so I could listen to it when I needed an energy boost. I guarantee it's a sure-fire way to get the party started!

I actually had a great time sampling all the versions available - from the TV show *Glee* version to the original *Dirty Dancing* movie version to the remix. I actually chose the Broadway production version as it had the best energy and I could sing along to it easily.

Take a few minutes to brainstorm about your Theme or Theme Song - write it down, try it on, revise or adjust it, sample some potential Theme songs, sing along to them - then we'll continue...

ABOUT BEGINNINGS AND Endings:

For many people, beginnings &/or endings are uncomfortable. The philosopher Seneca said, "Every new beginning comes from some other beginning's end."

But our human lives are filled with beginnings and endings - joined together by middles. They overlap, they create Venn diagrams (overlapping circles which visually represent the relationships between different yet connected ideas, people, projects or whatever).

They remind us that everything and everyone in our lives and our world is linked together, at least by the air we breathe. (What happened due to COVID-19 certainly taught us about that!)

You generally choose the beginnings and also the endings in your life, and every step in between, even when it seems you're being carried along by circumstance, fate or destiny. Your future is shaped by your past – your choices and actions—and there's always a **new beginning** up ahead!

9 ~ Empowering Your Future

It's time to do more inner-shifting by **Empowering Your Future!** This will help align you internally with where you are already heading, and get your subconscious onboard so it won't slow you down.

Let your Future guide you to the support systems, people, choices, opportunities and breakthroughs that will move you forward in a big way all year long.

ONCE AGAIN, SET ASIDE some time where you won't be disturbed so you can take full advantage of this fun and empowering process! Make an appointment with you Future Self and don't let anything get in the way.

If you've taken a break since we inner-journeyed to your Past in a previous episode, turn off your phones and shut your door to have all the privacy and quiet you need.

This will be a familiar journey by now, and you may find it much easier to travel forward than backward on your Timeline.

AS BEFORE, YOU CAN read the following meditation process to yourself as you go through it &/or record it for playback:

Close your eyes and get comfortable again...

Take some deep breaths and let yourself "just be" in this moment.

Now reconnect with your inner Timeline - **sense your Past direction and your Future direction again.**

Float up and move over your FUTURE TIMELINE now.

Notice many bright pearls containing Accomplishments and Learnings that can occur throughout the coming year appearing on your Timeline. They might already be there, or they may pop in as you float over them...

Float down now to a pearl several months ahead that draws your attention or glows brighter than the rest.

Trust that whichever pearl you choose is the right one - it can't be wrong, as *they're each potential experiences and aspects of your life to come!*

Look down into the glowing pearl and notice what's happening there...

- When and where is this event taking place...
- Who's there with you...
- How do you look and sound?

Now float back toward Now and pause above another pearl that's closer to Today - only a month or so ahead.

In that pearl, see yourself getting a phone call from someone who tells you about something that can make a difference in what you'll be doing over the rest of the coming year. It may be related to something you're already planning, or it may be something totally new and unexpected.

Don't question it - take whatever comes to mind...

As you look into the month-ahead pearl, notice where you are - and who is calling you. It may be someone you know today or someone you don't know yet.

- What does this person say?
- What do you say back?
- What do you do after you hang up the phone?
- What happens next?

WHEN YOU'RE READY TO move on, float gently upward and then forward over your *Future Timeline*.

Notice another pearl that's much closer to the end of the coming year.

Pause over it and see yourself within it.

Take a few moments to observe and absorb what's transpired for you in only one year.

Where are you... who's there with you... what are you wearing... what are you doing?

How are you feeling: confident, happy, calm, excited, busy or.......

What do you notice or learn by watching yourself in this Potential Future a year from now?

What's different for you - *or about you* - in this Future?

How do you feel about this Potential Future scene?

What can you do to make it occur the way you want it?

WHEN YOU'RE READY, float back over your Timeline to NOW and return to TODAY.

Let all the learnings from this inner journey absorb gently and easily into your energy field as you BREATHE...

NOW LOOK DOWN AT YOUR Future Timeline from Now and feel the year ahead of you as if it's already complete - you've read the book, seen the movie, know what's going to happen in the final chapter of your coming year.

Think about what's needed to make your story unfold from here to there *the way you want it.*

What steps can you take NOW - or soon - to direct the action where and how you want it to go?

What can you be prepared for in case surprises or challenges arise?

How do you want to "be" so you can handle whatever happens?

Take a deep breath and let the sense of YOUR STORY UNFOLDING settle into your energy field.

Know that your unique personal story is unfolding PERFECTLY. It always has been and it always will be...

You may not know the ending of your personal story yet - you won't know that until your life is complete - but you can imagine and envision where you're going from here, from today.

The Past is past, the Future's not yet known - all you ever have is the Present. Embrace it... empower it. Let it take you where you want to go...

***NOW TAKE 3 DEEP BREATHS** to gently bring you back into your body... into your personal space and time.*

When you're ready, open your eyes and return...

In your notebook, jot down any notes about what you saw or experienced during this part of your inner journey - especially anything that was new, insightful, surprising or meaningful for you.

WELCOME BACK! YOU'VE seen The Future from a Super-Conscious altitude.

Did you enjoy your visualization and Inner Journey into your Future? Did you discover some Future Accomplishment Pearls on your Timeline? Were you surprised by any of the future potentials - people, projects, opportunities, places, ideas - that shimmered within some of your bright pearls?

You have the power to shape your Future. By envisioning some potential Future Accomplishments, you've given them energy to magnetize the people, opportunities and resources into your life that can help them become real in a good way.

Your imagination and positive energy pave the way for you to get there from here. Know that your Future Timeline is always full of "potentials" - nothing is locked in stone or "destined" in ways you can't adjust or change through your free will and imagination. You're always moving forward - evolving - shifting - learning - and shaping the Future day by day! All you need to do is BE YOU - and enjoy the surprises that show up from now on.

10 ~ Enhancing Your RSN Journey with Creative Actions & More

Here are some ways you can work with the Ready Set Next processes whenever you need a fresh start or ongoing:

1 ~ JOURNALING:

Getting your thoughts out of your head and onto paper makes them tangible, gives them weight. This enables you to edit, revise, improve and change them.

If you keep a diary or do daily journaling, you can also use it to record your meditation notes.

If not, you can make notes on your computer. Be sure to name and date the file(s) so you can find them easily when you get ready to do your next Year Review!

In your journal, you can make sections for EMBRACING THE PAST & EMPOWERING THE FUTURE

As you work with the Past Timeline Meditations, be sure to have a journal, notebook or computer file ready for notes:

On separate pages, list these CATEGORY headings - fill in the blanks as you work with each of the meditations

WORD OR THEME FOR THE PAST YEAR
(or whatever time period you're working on)

YOUR PAST ACHIEVEMENTS & ACCOMPLISHMENTS
(These can include business, income, promotion, referrals, health, fun, relationships, environment, travel, contributions to others, lessons learned, insights, appreciation, etc.)

YOUR UNFINISHED BUSINESS
(These can include business, projects, income, health, relationships, environment, to-dos, "should have done's," unspoken communications, unreturned calls, unset emails, etc.)

EMPOWERING THE FUTURE
As you work with the Future Timeline Meditations, be sure to have a journal, notebook or computer file ready for notes:

WORD OR THEME FOR THE NEXT YEAR (or whatever time period you're working on)

EMPOWERING VISIONS & FEELINGS - By (specify date) I will:

(Write about where do you want to be; what are you doing, who's with you, how are you feeling – vision what's happening in business, health, family and other relationships, environment, travel, contributions to others, insights/lessons learned, appreciation, accomplishments, achievements)

YOUR S.M.A.R.T. GOALS:

(Write your goal in one sentence make it specific, measurable, achievable, realistic, time-based.)

YOUR FIRST STEPS INTO THE FUTURE - BY (specify date) I WILL:

(Write out your first steps - take as much space as you need.)

2 ~ WORKING IN A GROUP OR WITH A BUDDY:

If you like working on creative or personal improvement projects in a group, enlist a few friends to do these processes with you.

Find or create a Ready Set Next buddy or group for accountability, support, inspiration and cheerleading. It's always empowering to have someone else rooting for you - and to do it for each other.

You can also have a buddy or someone in your RSN support group who's a good reader be the one to read the meditations out loud, for you &/or everyone in the group.

Then you can also do this for them as well and receive the positive energy generated by supporting someone else to create a fresh start for themselves.

3 ~ COLLAGES & VISION BOARDS:

You might also create a Ready Set Next COLLAGE or Vision Board with clippings of images that represent your Past Accomplishments &/or Future Accomplishments and Opportunities.

Images can be found in magazines and clipped or you can find images online, print them out, and paste them on your Board (or on a virtual board if you prefer to go paperless).

You can do this all in one day or gradually, adding more images to your Vision Board as you find them. Or you can host an RSN Vision Board PARTY with friends or your support group buddies and do it together.

Put your Vision Board where you can see it every day. If it's a Past Accomplishments board, let it remind you that the energy of your Accomplishments now lives within you. It helps to empower you to attract new opportunities, people and accomplishments as you move forward today and into your Future.

If it's a Future Accomplishments board, add to it or adjust it as needed to help make your vision tangible as your future unfolds.

You could make one board for career or work or your business; one for your relationships &/or romance &/or family; one for travel; one for health and self-care. You can make a whole wall of Visions to reflect your Inner Journey unfolding day by day, month by month, year by year.

back to school in her 50s and 60s for training as a Certified Hypnotherapist, a life/career breakthrough coach, and an Akashic Records Advanced Teacher and Healing Practitioner.

Her articles on life balance and spiritual/personal growth have been published in magazines and online. She also has chapters in a dozen book anthologies and has published several solo-written books on life balance and spiritual evolution.

Barbara's life-journey led her from a Chicago childhood to a Hollywood career in story development where she worked with A-list Hollywood talent, TV networks and studios.

While learning to balance her own life and raise a world-traveling daughter with her husband of 40+ years Glenn Schiffman (also a writer and spiritual coach), Barbara's had numerous exhilarating experiences. She completed marathons (despite hating to exercise), walked on hot coals with Tony Robins, and taken countless leaps of faith. She also co-founded the first Toastmasters Int'l chapter in Los Angeles CA designed to help writers become better speakers.

She now lives in Northwest Montana with Glenn to be close to their daughter and twin grandsons. She continues to mentor writers, support spiritual seekers, and take leaps of faith.

Read more at https://LiteraSee.com.